# SNAKES

# BOA CONSTRICTORS

## James E. Gerholdt
### ABDO & Daughters

Published by Abdo & Daughters, 4940 Viking Drive, Suite 622, Edina, Minnesota 55435.

Library bound edition distributed by Rockbottom Books, Pentagon Tower, P.O. Box 36036, Minneapolis, Minnesota 55435.

Printed in the United States.

Cover Photo credit: Peter Arnold, Inc.
Interior Photo credits: Peter Arnold, Inc. pages 7, 9, 11, 13, 15, 17, 21
Jim Gerholdt, pages 5, 19

**Edited by Julie Berg**

### Library of Congress Cataloging-in-Publication Data

Gerholdt, James E., 1943
    Boa constrictors / James E. Gerholdt.
      p. cm. — (Snakes)
Includes bibliographical references (p. 23) and index.
ISBN 1-56239-513-0 *15/7*
1. Boa constrictor—Juvenile literature. [1. Boa constrictor. 2. Snakes.] I. Title. II.
Series: Gerholdt, James E., 1943- Snakes.
QL666.063G473     1995
597.96—dc20                      95-18607
                                      CIP
                                       AC

### About the Author

Jim Gerholdt has been studying reptiles and amphibians for more than 40 years. He has presented lectures and displays throughout the state of Minnesota for 9 years. He is a founding member of the Minnesota Herpetological Society and is active in conservation issues involving reptiles and amphibians in India and Aruba, as well as Minnesota.

Revised Edition 2002

# Contents

BOA CONSTRICTORS ............................ 4

SIZES ................................................. 6

COLORS .............................................. 8

WHERE THEY LIVE ............................. 10

WHERE THEY ARE FOUND .................. 12

SENSES ............................................. 14

DEFENSE ........................................... 16

FOOD ................................................ 18

BABIES .............................................. 20

GLOSSARY ......................................... 22

BIBLIOGRAPHY ................................... 23

INDEX ................................................ 24

# BOA CONSTRICTORS

Boa constrictors belong to one of the 11 families of snakes. They are divided into several **subspecies**.

A snake is a **reptile**, which is a **vertebrate**. This means they have a backbone, just like a human.

Boas are **cold blooded.** They get their body temperature from lying in the sun, on a warm log, or the warm ground. If they are too cool, their bodies won't work. If they are too hot, they will die.

They are called boa constrictors because they kill their food by **constricting** it. That means they wrap around their **prey** and squeeze it until it **suffocates**.

*A boa constrictor is a reptile, which is a vertebrate.*
*This means it has a backbone.*

# SIZES

The boa constrictor is a large snake with a heavy body. The size of the adult depends on its **subspecies**. The length of a boa constrictor is measured from the tip of the nose to the tip of the tail.

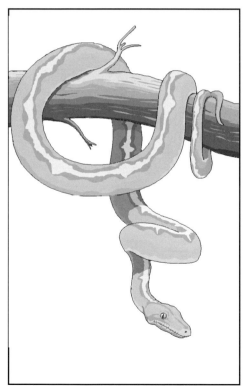

The Mexican boa constrictor averages four to five feet (1.2 to 1.5 m) in length. The largest ones average eight feet (2.4 m) in length.

The largest boa constrictor ever found came from Trinidad. It measured 18.5 feet (5.6 m) long.

*The boa constrictor is a large snake with a heavy body.*

# COLORS

Boa constrictors have dark brown blotches on a light tan or buff colored background. Some, like the red-tailed boas, have red blotches on their tails. Others, such as the Argentine boa constrictor, are much darker, with a dark brown background. The Hog Island boa constrictor has blotches that are almost as light as the background.

No matter how light or dark, the boa constrictor's colors help it to blend in with its surroundings. This is called **camouflage**.

*Most boa constrictors have dark brown blotches on a light tan or buff colored background.*

# WHERE THEY LIVE

Boa constrictors are found in many different **habitats**. People think boas are always found in jungles and **rainforests**. Some are, but they are also found in desert areas without many trees.

Boa constrictors usually live on the ground. But since they are good climbers, they are sometimes found in trees. Young boas are more likely than adults to make their way up a tree.

Boas will use **mammal burrows** and hollow logs as hiding places. They all have their own place in the world.

*Boa constrictors are often found in rainforests and jungles.*

# WHERE THEY ARE FOUND

Boa constrictors live in Mexico, Central America, and South America. They are also found on the Lesser Antilles' many small islands, including Trinidad, Tobago, and Dominica.

*This boa constrictor is from Brazil in South America.*

The Argentine boa constrictor is found the farthest south, in Paraguay and Argentina. The Peruvian boa constrictor is found only in Peru.

# SENSES

Boa constrictors and humans have four of the same senses. Boas have trouble seeing anything that isn't moving. Their **pupils** are **vertical**, which helps them to see in the dark, when much of their activity takes place. These vertical pupils open up in the dark to let in more light.

Like all snakes, boa constrictors don't have ears and cannot hear. But they can feel **vibrations** through bones in the lower jaw.

Their most important sense is smell. All snakes use their tongue with which to smell. Without the tongue, a boa constrictor could not find its food.

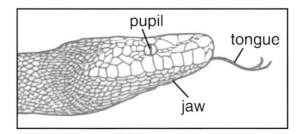

*Boa constrictors have trouble seeing*
*anything that isn't moving.*

# DEFENSE

The boa constrictor's coloring helps it blend in with its surroundings. This **camouflage** is their most important defense against enemies such as crocodiles, jungle cats, and humans. If the enemy can't see it, the boa constrictor is safe.

If an enemy does find it, the boa may try to crawl to a safe place. If this doesn't work, it will **coil**, open its mouth, and make a very loud hissing noise. It will also bite!

Because the teeth of a boa constrictor are sharp like needles, the bite will hurt, even though there is no **venom**. The bite is not dangerous to humans.

*The boa constrictor's coloring helps it blend in with its surroundings.*

# FOOD

A hungry boa constrictor will eat any bird or **mammal** it can swallow whole. They also eat **iguanas**.

The boa will keep still, hidden by its **camouflage**. When an animal comes close, it will strike out and grab the **prey** with its mouth, using its sharp teeth to hold on. The boa will then **coil** around the animal and **constrict** it.

The constriction doesn't crush or break any bones, like some people think. Constriction **suffocates** the prey. Once the animal is dead, the boa swallows it, usually head first!

*A boa constrictor eating a mouse.*

# BABIES

Boa constrictors give birth to live young. The females can have twenty to more than fifty babies. The larger the female, the more babies she will have.

The size of the babies depends on the size of the mother. The average size at birth is about twenty inches (51 cm) long.

The babies shed their skin for the first time at the age of seven to ten days. This shedding is called **ecdysis**. Now the babies are ready to hunt for food. As they grow, they continue to shed the old skin.

*This young boa constrictor is shedding its skin.*

# GLOSSARY

**Burrow** - A hole dug in the ground by an animal for shelter or protection.

**Camouflage** (CAM-a-flaj) - The ability to blend in with the surroundings.

**Coil** - To roll or twist into a loop.

**Cold-blooded** - Animals that get their body temperature from an outside source.

**Constrict** (kun-STRICK) - To squeeze or compress together.

**Ecdysis** (ek-DIE-sis) - The process of shedding the old skin.

**Geographic** (gee-a-GRAFF-ik) - Different areas of the Earth.

**Habitat** (HAB-uh-tat) - An area in which an animal lives.

**Iguana** (ih-GWAH-nah) - A large green lizard that lives in the same areas as boa constrictors.

**Mammals** (MAM-alls) - Warm-blooded animals with backbones that nurse their young.

**Mammal burrows** - Holes dug by mammals.

**Prey** - An animal that is hunted for food.

**Pupil** (PEW-pill) - The center part of the iris, or the dark center of the colored part of the eye.

**Rainforest** - A very thick forest in a place where rain is very heavy all through the year.

**Reptile** - A scaly-skinned animal with a backbone.

**Subspecies** (SUB-spee-seas) - A geographic race of a species.

**Suffocate** - To kill by stopping breathing.
**Venom** (VEN-um) - Poison that is used to kill animals for food.
**Vertebrate** (VER-tuh-brit) - An animal with a backbone.
**Vertical** (VERT-i-kull) - Up and down.
**Vibration** (vie-BRAY-shun) - A quivering or trembling motion.

# BIBLIOGRAPHY

Coborn, John. *The Atlas of Snakes of the World*. T.F.H. Publications, Inc., 1991.

Mattison, Chris. *Snakes of the World*. Facts On File, Inc., 1986.

Mehrtens, John M. *Living Snakes of the World in Color*. Sterling Publishing Company, 1987.

Obst, Fritz Jurgen, Klaus Richter, and Udo Jacob. *The Completely Illustrated Atlas of Reptiles and Amphibians for the Terrarium*. T.F.H. Publications, Inc., 1988.

Pope, Clifford H. *The Giant Snakes*. Alfred A. Knopf, 1965.

# Index

## A

Argentina  13
Argentine boa
    constrictor 8,  13

## B

babies  20
backbone  4
bird  18
birth  20
blotches  8
boa constrictor,
    female 20
bodies  6
body temperature
    4
bones 14, 18
burrows 10

## C

camouflage
    8, 16, 18
Central
    America 12
climbing 10
coil 16, 18
cold blooded 4
color 8, 16
constriction 4, 18

## D

defense 16
desert areas  10
Dominica  12

## E

ears  14
ecdysis  20
enemies  16
eyes  14
eyesight  14

## F

family 4
food 4, 14, 18, 20

## H

habitats 10
hearing 14
hissing 16
Hog Island boa
    constrictor  8
human 4, 14, 16
hunt 20

## I

iguana  18

## J

jaw  14
jungle  10

## L

length 6
Lesser Antilles
    12
logs 10
lower jaw  14

## M

mammal  10, 18
mammal burrows
    10
Mexican boa
    constrictor  6
Mexico  12
mouth 16, 18

## P

Paraguay  13
Peru  13
Peruvian boa
    constrictor  13
prey 4, 18
pupil 14

## R

rainforest  10
red-tailed boas  8
reptile  4

## S

senses  14
shedding 20
sight 14
size 6, 20
skin 20
smell 14
South America
    12
subspecies
    4, 6, 8
suffocation 4, 18
sun  4

## T

tail 6, 8
teeth  16, 18
Tobago  12
tongue  14
trees 10
Trinidad 6, 12

## V

venom  16
vertebrate  4
vibrations 14